Photography

ART TODAY!

Photography

Sara James

Mason Crest

Mason Crest
450 Parkway Drive, Suite D
Broomall, PA 19008
www.masoncrest.com

Printed and bound in the United States of America.

First printing
9 8 7 6 5 4 3 2 1

Series ISBN: 978-1-4222-3167-8
ISBN: 978-1-4222-3175-3
ebook ISBN: 978-1-4222-8712-5

Library of Congress Cataloging-in-Publication Data

James, Sara, author.
  Photography / Sara James.
      pages cm. — (Art today!)
  Audience: Age 12+.
  Audience: Grades 7 to 8.
  Includes bibliographical references and index.
  ISBN 978-1-4222-3175-3 (hardback) — ISBN 978-1-4222-3167-8 (series) — ISBN 978-1-4222-8712-5 (ebook) 1. Photography—Juvenile literature. 2. Photography—Digital techniques—Juvenile literature. 3. Photography—History—Juvenile literature. I. Title.
  TR149.J34 2015
  770—dc23
                                                    2014011831

Contents

KEY ICONS TO LOOK FOR:

 Text-Dependent Questions: These questions send the reader back to the text for more careful attention to the evidence presented there.

 Words to Understand: These words with their easy-to-understand definitions will increase the reader's understanding of the text, while building vocabulary skills.

 Series Glossary of Key Terms: This back-of-the book glossary contains terminology used throughout this series. Words found here increase the reader's ability to read and comprehend higher-level books and articles in this field.

 Research Projects: Readers are pointed toward areas of further inquiry connected to each chapter. Suggestions are provided for projects that encourage deeper research and analysis.

Sidebars: This boxed material within the main text allows readers to build knowledge, gain insights, explore possibilities, and broaden their perspectives by weaving together additional information to provide realistic and holistic perspectives.

Words to Understand

amateur: Someone who doesn't get paid for something, who does it as a hobby.

professional: Someone who gets paid to do something for a living.

medium: A material used by an artist to create a work of art. Clay, paint, sound are all different kinds of media.

spontaneous: Happening without planning.

accessories: Things that can be added to something else to make it more useful.

physics: The science behind the energy, matter, motion, and force of the things that make up our universe.

chemistry: The science of how atoms and molecules interact.

prism: A transparent piece of glass or plastic that changes the light that passes through it in some way.

composition: The way the things in a photograph are arranged.

sophisticated: Complicated or advanced.

pristine: Flawless or perfect.

controversial: The subject of much argument and debate.

Chapter One

Creating Photographs

If you decide to start taking photographs, you'll find you have a lot of choices these days. You can snap a quick photo on your phone, or you can use your computer or tablet to take a decent picture. Maybe you have a digital camera or even a film camera to capture some images.

From a once-in-a-while activity to a hobby to a professional business, photography helps us take a closer look at the world. And it's an art form that just about anyone can create, as long as she has some sort of camera.

FILM PHOTOGRAPHY

Photographers have two main choices about how to take pictures. They can decide to go digital, or they can choose to use film. Film is the older

If you have a passion for taking photographs, you can turn your love of photography into a full-time career with a bit of hard work and education.

way of taking pictures—and it was the only choice for a long time—but both **amateur** and **professional** photographers continue to use this **medium**.

Film photography forces the photographer to think more about each photo before he takes it. Each roll of film usually holds only twenty-four or thirty-six chances to take a picture before the roll runs out. Meanwhile, digital photographers can take thousands of pictures before space runs out on the camera and discard the pictures they don't like. Many photographers, however, like the slower, more careful pace that film photography creates.

To take photographs from film, you first need a film camera! Companies still make film cameras, but lots of photographers choose to use old film cameras, some made in the 1970s or before. Old film cameras tend to be very well made. They have stood the test of time.

Most film cameras are 35 mm. That means the film they use is 35 millimeters wide. These are the least expensive cameras, which use the least-expensive film. Photographers load the film spool into the camera, and then wind it up to feed in the roll.

Other cameras are large-format machines. The take much bigger pictures than the standard 35 mm camera, and they are better for taking close-up pictures when you have a lot of time to stage a shot. They aren't very good for **spontaneous** images, though. Large-format cameras use 4-by-5-inch film sheets that must be loaded one by one into the camera.

Film cameras allow photographers to control the exposure, which changes the photographs that turn out in the end. Exposure is the amount of light that's allowed to hit the film. It's controlled by two settings called aperture and shutter speed. To figure out how to properly set them, you'll need to practice!

Aperture is how wide the lens opening is. It affects what is in focus in the picture being taken. When the lens is open just a little bit, only a little light is let through, while wider openings let in more light. Aperture is measured in f-stops. Smaller f-stops actually mean a wider aperture, which can get confusing at first. To get a picture in which everything is in focus, use a smaller aperture. A wider aperture is better for close-ups or when you're only focusing on one object that's quite close to you.

Shutter speed also controls how much light reaches the film. A fast shutter speed indicates the picture is taken really fast, while a slow shutter speed means the lens is open for longer to allow in more light. Faster shutter speeds are good when there's a lot of light around, and when you're taking pictures of moving objects. Otherwise, your photo might turn out blurry, unless you're using a tripod to keep the camera steady. (A tripod is a three-legged stand for a camera that holds a camera still during the shot.)

Photographers can choose from a wide range of **accessories** to add to their cameras. They can attach lenses that let them zoom in on tiny subjects. They can buy different sorts of flashes to get the light in their pictures just right.

Film photographers also often enjoy developing their photographs themselves. After taking a roll of pictures, they go through the process of developing the film into negatives, and then printing pictures from those negatives. If you're interested in developing your own pictures, you'll need access to a darkroom. Because film and photo paper is very light sensitive, they need to be handled in a special room that blocks out light.

Developing images from film takes a few hours and several steps. Here is the basic outline for film development:

1. Thread the used-up film onto a reel that allows it to develop into negatives. You'll first need to open up a full film canister. This must be done in complete darkness. Then cut off the ends of the film and spool it onto a special plastic or metal reel that loops the film around and around without letting any part touch any other part. Load it into a film tank that doesn't allow any light in.

2. Develop the film. This can be done in the light, since the tank protects your film. You'll dunk the film tank into a series of chemicals that develop the images hidden on the film. First you'll dunk it in the developer, then the stop bath, the fixer, and water. The

specific chemicals are different depending on whether you're developing color or black-and-white film.

3. Dry the film and then load it into binders to protect it until you want to create photographs.

4. Develop the pictures from the film in a darkroom. First, use a special machine called an enlarger to project an image from a negative onto photo paper. The enlarger has a light on it, which is the only time your photo will be exposed to light before it's done. The photo will turn out differently depending on how long it is exposed to light, and how much light you let in. Like with the film, you'll next dunk the photo paper into several different chemicals, again called developer, stop bath, and fixer, followed by water. Let it dry.

Those might seem like a lot of steps, but film photographers think all the

Make Connections

 Disposable cameras used to be very popular, but digital cameras and phones have mostly replaced them. If you can find one to buy, though, they're fun to play around with. They offer a good introduction to film cameras if you don't want to start off by buying an expensive film camera right away. You don't need to feed film into disposable cameras—you simply wind up the camera, point, and click—and then, when you've take all the shots, mail the entire camera away to get the film processed.

You might even find an old Polaroid camera stashed away somewhere, which allows you to take pictures and see them instantly. Not many places produce Polaroid film anymore, but you can still order it online. Modern photographers are increasingly interested in using Polaroid cameras as an art form.

Understanding the difference between film and digital photography can help you to use the right tool for the art you want to make.

work is well worth the results. They have control over every step along the way, allowing them to create unique works of art.

THE SCIENCE OF FILM PHOTOGRAPHY

Film photography is an art, but it also has a lot to do with science! Film cameras depend on the laws of **physics** and **chemistry** to produce images.

When you take a picture, you are basically letting light into a box. The camera lens focuses and directs the light onto the film. The lens actually flips the image upside down and from right to left. Cameras have a **prism** inside that re-flips the image so that it looks like it does out in the world. Only a certain amount of light is let into the camera, because the camera shutter opens and closes. The amount of light affects the picture you'll get at the end.

Each color of light that reaches the film causes a chemical reaction to happen to the materials coating the film. When you develop the film, you expose the hidden image created by the reactions. Each chemical used in the process does something different. The developer converts the chemical reactions into the image. The stop bath stops the developer from working past a certain point. The fixer makes the image permanent and keeps it stable when it's eventually exposed to light again. The film produces a negative image—one where all the dark areas of an object appear light, and all the light images appear dark. Developing photographs from the negative reverses the image to become positive again.

Developing the photo on paper is very similar. You project the negative onto photo paper, which is coated with light-sensitive chemicals. When you shine light through the negative, you make chemical reactions happen on the paper. By dunking the paper into the developer, stop bath, and fixer, you go through the whole process again, this time producing the final picture.

From cameras in smartphones to advanced digital cameras, digital photography has almost entirely replaced film photography for many amateur photographers.

DIGITAL PHOTOGRAPHY

While film cameras are still around, most photographers now use digital cameras, especially amateur ones. Digital photography can mean everything from taking pictures with a smartphone to using an expensive, tricked-out digital camera.

Digital photography allows you to take lots of pictures at once without fear that you're wasting film. Digital cameras usually allow the people using them to control more things when taking the picture, and some provide editing tools right on screen.

For beginning photographers, or people who just want to capture life's moments, digital cameras have automatic modes. You don't need to know how to adjust for lighting—you just need to point and click.

For more advanced photographers, digital cameras also often offer lots of manual settings. You can change the exposure based on how much light there is. As with film cameras, you can change both the aperture and the shutter speed.

You don't need a fancy, expensive camera to be a digital photographer. Some artists are using their iPhones to create works of art! There's even an annual iPhone photography contest. Phones have all sorts of photography apps that can boost your photos to the next level. And if you pay attention to things like light, **composition**, and zoom, you can take some great photos.

Taking the photos with a digital camera is only half the battle if you want polished works of art. Rather than the darkroom, digital photographers turn to image editing software on computers to finish up their photos. Software has multiple capabilities, from simple tools like cropping and straightening, to more complicated tools like changing colors and inserting new images into the photo.

Image editing software can save even fairly bad photos, depending on how **sophisticated** it is. Dark photos become lighter and easier to see, washed-out photos become brighter, and unwanted objects can be removed to leave a picture **pristine**.

Research Project

Do some research online to find another photographer besides Annie Liebovitz who has used both film and digital photography. Write a paragraph about this person's background. Then write a paragraph or two about what sort of pictures this photographer creates, and why he or she takes photos. Finally, write a paragraph about why the photographer switched from one type of photography to the other.

Photographers of all levels have a variety of software options. The most expensive will produce the best results but are often out of the price range for beginners. Photoshop is probably the best-known software, and it can do just about anything you can think of to images. Photoshop comes in different levels, including some beginner options. You can also search around online for cheaper or even free software.

BRIDGING THE GAP

Most amateur photographers use digital cameras, but artistic photographers these days often use both. Annie Liebovitz is an example of a photographer who has used both film and digital photography during her career. Liebovitz started out taking photographs for *Rolling Stone* magazine and later worked for *Vanity Fair*. She became famous for her portraits of celebrities. She managed to capture a lot of emotion and story in each picture she took. Some of her photographs were **controversial**, which made her even more famous.

For a long time, Liebovitz used film photography, since that's what was available. She mastered the use of lighting, film, and picture

Text-Dependent Questions

1. What are the two types of photography? Why might someone choose the first over the second? Or the second over the first?
2. How can photographers control the exposure on their cameras?
3. Why do film photographers have to use darkrooms?
4. What do each of the chemicals used in developing film do?
5. Name at least three things image-editing software allows photographers to do.

development. While Liebovitz still uses film photography today, she has been trying out digital more and more She started switching to digital photography and had her first all-digital photography show in 2012 at the Smithsonian American Art Museum in Washington, D.C. In an interview with the website Co.Create, she said, "I'm still learning about digital, the way we all are. In fact, some of the early work . . . I want to go back and redo now that the technology is better. Or maybe my eye is better." Liebovitz is making the most out of both photography worlds.

Words to Understand

innovative: Having to do with a new and original way of doing things.

aesthetic: Purely for the sake of beauty or how something looks.

intellectual: Having to do with thought and mental abilities.

mapping: The process of creating maps.

journalism: The news industry.

Chapter Two

The History
of Photography

Compared to other types of art, photography is pretty new. No one could practice this art form until the earliest cameras were developed. For a very long time, people couldn't capture images of the world as it actually looks. They could paint the world, or write and sing about it, but they couldn't photograph it. Today, art has expanded even more with the addition of photography.

EARLY PICTURES

The earliest cameras were a far cry from the cameras we have today, but they were *innovative* for their time. Many hundreds of years ago, people figured out that they could project images from the world onto

The camera obscura was the first kind of camera, but cameras have changed radically since the first advances in photography.

Make Connections

Photography is based on Greek words that mean "drawing with light." *Photo* means light, while *-graphy* signifies drawing or writing.

a flat surface using a camera obscura (also called a pinhole camera). The camera obscura was basically a box that was kept dark, with one hole in the side that let in light. Whatever was in front of the hole was projected into the box and onto the surface inside. People in China, Greece, and Byzantium all had some version of the camera obscura. However, no one had figured out how to make the image permanent. Artists mostly used the camera obscura to project images that they then traced for their drawings and paintings.

In the 1500s, a man named Daniello Barbaro realized that he could sharpen the image created by a camera obscura by putting a glass lens in the hole. The lens focused the light so that the image wasn't as fuzzy. This was an important discovery for later cameras.

Separately, other people discovered chemicals that changed when they were exposed to light. Silver nitrate mixed with chalk is one example. These chemicals held the key to making images permanent, but no one had tried to put the two discoveries together until the 1800s. At first, experimenters could capture an image from a camera obscura on glass covered in the light-sensitive chemicals, but the images faded quickly.

In 1835, William Henry Fox Talbot finally discovered a way to keep the images more permanently. At about the same time, Louis Daguerre was also experimenting with photography. Daguerre figured out a way

George Eastman has a star on the Hollywood Walk of Fame honoring his role in making photography and film what they are today.

to create permanent images while also reducing the exposure time from a few hours (or days!) to minutes. He used paper coated with silver iodide and developed the image with mercury fumes. Exposure to these chemicals made it a dangerous process by today's standards, but Daguerre spread his process around the world. Photographs using his method were called daguerreotypes.

Meanwhile, Talbot was still working hard on his own process. He invented a way to create a negative that could then produce many prints of one photo. It is the same basic method we use today with film cameras. Photos created with his method were called calotypes.

So far, photography was only for the professionals. Cameras were huge and came with portable darkrooms so the photographer could develop the image right away. Only people who were serious about photography bothered to take pictures. It would be a while before non-professionals had access to photography.

Early professional photographers were taking pictures of landscapes and people. Photographers often made their money taking portrait pictures of people who could afford the expensive early pictures. Wealthy people wanted to get in on the latest invention and capture images of themselves and their loved ones. As experimenters started to make photography better and cheaper, people who were not quite so wealthy could also afford to have their picture taken.

PHOTOGRAPHY FOR THE MASSES

Probably the person that did the most for photography is George Eastman. Eastman made photography an everyday activity. His company, Eastman Kodak, ruled the photography world for many decades. It sold film, cameras, camera equipment, and more.

Eastman was a Rochester, New York, businessman. In 1880, he invented the film sheet roll, which made taking pictures a whole lot easier. That same year, he set up a film shop in Rochester and it quickly took off. Before his invention, people had to take pictures one by one and

For many years, Kodak enjoyed huge success in film and cameras. In recent years, however, the company has fallen on hard times, having to all but stop making cameras and film as digital photography and phone cameras became more popular.

remove the film sheet after each picture. He created the now-familiar way to turn the film sheets into film rolls that advanced one by one until they were all used up.

Eastman didn't keep his invention to himself. He also developed a small, handheld camera that held this roll of film—and anyone could buy it, if they had the money. Once someone used up the film, she mailed the whole camera back to Eastman's company. The film was developed, and the prints and camera sent back to the owner.

Over time, Eastman Kodak refined the portable camera and the film that went with it. In 1900, the company introduced the Brownie camera. The Brownie was small, and most important, it was cheap: it cost only $1. While $1 was worth a lot more in 1900 than it's worth today, $1 was still affordable for many families who wanted a camera.

Eastman died in 1932, but his company kept on going strong for many years. A few years after Eastman's death, Kodak introduced color film. Meanwhile, other inventors were coming up with improved flash

Make Connections

Moving pictures go hand in hand with still images. Soon after the invention of the photograph, people started trying to apply the new technology to capture moving pictures. Thomas Edison captured the first moving pictures on film made by Eastman's company in 1889, using an invention called the Kinetograph. Other early filming methods included the Phantoscope, the Pleograph, and the Ciné-matograph created by the Lumiere brothers. Eventually, the technology led to full-length silent feature films, movies with sound, color film, and beyond.

bulbs, zoom lenses, the Polaroid camera, and more. It had never been so easy for average, everyday people to take pictures.

By the middle of the twentieth century, photography researchers were on to even newer things. In 1969, George Smith and Willard Boyle came up with the charge-coupled device (CCD). A CCD is a piece of equipment that senses images and is the basis for digital photography. A few years later, Sony introduced the first digital camera called the Mavica, which used CCD technology. The Mavica recorded images on a floppy disk and held twenty-five images per disk.

Kodak again took the lead in photography with digital cameras, but not for long. One early Kodak digital camera cost $30,000! Lots of other companies focused on digital technology and came out with cheaper and better cameras. The Apple QuickTake camera was the first digital camera that people could use at home; it could hook up to a home computer. Fuji and Canon were also entering the field.

The first digital cameras just looked like big boxes. Then they looked like slightly smaller, wide, flat boxes. Over time, CCDs got smaller and smaller, until companies could produce tiny digital cameras that looked a lot like film cameras. An alternative image sensor called active pixel CMOS sensors made digital cameras cheaper. And today, digital photographic technology is an everyday part of other electronic devices, especially phones.

THE ART OF PHOTOGRAPHY

All the inventions that led up to the modern camera paved the way for photography as art. Sure, people could use cameras to record pictures of their family and vacations, but they could also use them to create works of art meant for more than just remembering moments. Photographs could use representations of the real world to make people think more deeply about things.

Most people define art as something a person has created to evoke emotions in others (good or bad). It is created for purely **aesthetic** or **intellectual** reasons rather than practical ones. In other words, art has no use except to be looked at. When photography first began, people mainly used it for more practical purposes. Today, we still use photography for practical things like **mapping** and **journalism**, but we also take pictures for artistic reasons.

At first, photography struggled to be accepted as art. People thought it wasn't as good or noble as older forms of art, such as painting. In the 1800s, some people interested in photography formed photographic societies. These societies were made up of both professionals and amateurs. Some of them were focused on promoting photography as an art form.

Over time, people began to accept that photography could be art just as much as painting or sculpture. Today, photography is featured in art shows, museums, and on walls around the world. Art history includes photography. You can take photography art classes.

One famous and fairly early art photographer is Ansel Adams. Adams was a black-and-white landscape photographer. Landscape photographers take pictures of the outdoors, including mountains, lakes, forests, cities, and more.

Photographers enjoy taking pictures, but many professional photographers also use their art form for a specific cause. Some may photograph a particular group of people who they want others to pay attention to. Other photographers capture images of places they want saved.

ANSEL ADAMS

Adams is an example of an art photographer with a mission. His mission was to preserve the landscapes he loved, to protect them from development. Adams photographed dramatic landscapes to convince his audience that the places he loved deserved to be saved.

Research Project

Do some research in action! You can make your own camera obscura, just like the very first photographers. You'll need a metal can (like a coffee can) or a cardboard container (round oatmeal containers work well). One end should be open to the air. If there are any holes in your container besides the open end, tape them up with duct tape. Next, poke a hole in the end opposite the open end using a hammer and nail. Then cover up the open end of the container with wax paper, securing it with a rubber band. Now cover yourself and the wax paper end of the container with a blanket, but leave the end with the hole uncovered. Point that end toward an object or scene that is brightly lit, like out a window during the day. Under your blanket, you should see the same object projected upside down onto the wax paper. Do some reading online to figure out why exactly this happens and write up your findings. Also explain what would happen if you put a glass lens in the hole.

Adams grew up in California. He started to teach himself photography after he visited Yosemite National Park as a young person. His early love of landscapes suck with him throughout his life. His passion for landscapes was also influenced by the fact that his grandfather and father owned a lumber business. Rather than following in his family's destructive footsteps, he decided he wanted to preserve forests.

In the 1940s, Adams switched gears a little. He still photographed landscapes, but he also took pictures of the social injustices he saw in the country. In the 1940s, he visited Japanese internment camps in the Southwest. Many Japanese immigrants and Japanese-Americans were imprisoned in these camps during World War II, when the United States

Text-Dependent Questions

1. How did the addition of a lens help make images produced by the camera obscura better?
2. What were the first two types of permanent photographic images called and how were they different? Who invented each one?
3. What was George Eastman's first photographic invention, and how did it change the world of photography?
4. What is a CCD and how did it affect photography?
5. How did Ansel Adams use photography to bring attention to his personal mission?

was fighting Japan. Adams believed this was a terrible injustice, and he took pictures of life in the camps, to spread awareness of what was going on. He used his art form to do more than just take pictures of beautiful landscapes and people. His photos opened people's minds to new truths.

Words to Understand

passion: Something someone cares about very strongly.
apprentice: Someone studying under an expert to learn to be very good at something.

Chapter Three

The Business
of Photography

Photography can be a lot of things—it can be an art, a way to preserve memories, a hobby, and even a business. Some photographers just can't imagine life without taking pictures, so they turn their *passion* into a living. Running a photography business and making enough money to live on is hard work. It requires some luck, along with skill. But some people make it happen, and they are glad to get a chance to do something they love so much.

MAKING THE DECISION

A few people stumble on starting up a photography business. Maybe they've been practicing photography as a hobby and they have a friend

Picking one kind of photograph (such as nature photography) may help your chances of having success in the world of photography.

with a photography business who invites them to join. More likely, they have to start a business from scratch. Photographers who want to start making money from their hobby need to make a decision to start a business.

Most people who start photography businesses have been taking pictures for a while. They've gotten really good at taking pictures and have often focused on one specific kind of photography. Some really like taking nature pictures or pictures of kids or they like making works of art that really make people think. Each sort of photography can become its own business, but the process of starting and running the business might be a little different, depending on the type of photography.

TYPES OF BUSINESSES

Photographers can choose from a wide range of business types, based on what kind of photography interests them. Making money as

Make Connections

Stock photography supplies photographs to users for specific purposes. Companies buy the pictures instead of hiring a photographer. Today, stock images can found in searchable online databases. They can be purchased and delivered online. Often, these photographs involve people and are produced in studios using models who pose as various kinds of professionals, expressing common emotions and gestures. Some stock photography includes animals or images related to travel and tourism, as well as conceptual photography. Advertising agencies, publishers, magazines, and all sorts of businesses can purchase these photos, often at a fairly cheap price.

There are a wide variety of stock photography websites that allow photographers to sell their work online. Putting your work on these sites can be a good way to make a bit of money and share your photos with others.

Selling your own work at a festival or fair can be a good way to make money with your photography.

a photographer can be hard, especially when you're just starting out. With some creativity and a willingness to do whatever it takes, a new photographer will be on her way to a successful business.

Lots of photographers take stock photos. Businesses buy stock photos to use in their ads, on their websites, or in their publications. They don't want to hire a professional photographer to take the few pictures they need, so they buy stock photos online that match what they're looking for.

Starting a business can take your photography career to the next level.

Photographers can take stock photos of just about anything—people, places, textures, animals, and more. Some photographers take pictures of everything, while others focus on just one particular subject, like kids, and get really good at it so that more people will end up buying their photos.

If you're interested in contributing to a stock photo website, go check them out to see the quality of photos required, and to get an idea of the price for which you can sell them. Fotolia, iStockPhoto, Dreamstime, and Getty Images are all popular stock photo sites. Once you think you're ready, you'll need to submit an application and some of your photos to the site so they can be evaluated. If you pass the test, you'll be able to upload your images. Every time someone buys one, you'll make a little money.

Artistic photographers specifically try to sell their photography as art. They show their work in art galleries, where each piece is for sale. Some cities have open-studio nights that allow artists to showcase their art. Coffee shops, restaurants, and other small businesses sometimes have a rotating art display to highlight local artists. If photographers can hang their pictures in one of these places, lots of people will see their art—and they might even sell a few pieces. Photographers' websites are other useful platforms to sell prints individually to customers.

Make Connections

Artists aren't the only ones who work in the field of art. There are lots of other people, like museum curators, gallery owners, art critics, art collectors, and equipment sellers. All these people matter when it comes to turning art into a business, so it's good to get to know a few!

Different photographers will find different ways to support themselves with their photography, from wedding photos to magazine photoshoots.

If you want to make a name for yourself as a photographer, think about entering photo contests so that people start to notice your work. If your photos are good enough and you start winning, you could catch the eye of someone who could help you start to make money as an artist.

Another option is to sell your work at arts-and-crafts events. At these events, artists and crafters set up individual booths to show off their wares. This is a good way to get a large group of potential customers looking at art all at once. Visit any arts-and-crafts show, and you'll probably find some photographers there. Many of them are very good. They enjoy interacting with customers and talking about their art.

Some photographers start their own event photo businesses. People need photographers to take pictures of weddings, birthdays, retirement parties, and other big events. There are a lot of event photographers out there though, so each one works hard to stand out from the crowd.

Not all photographers are just involved in taking pictures and trying to sell them. Some also work with photographic equipment. There are fewer film photography stores these days, but there are still some around. You can often find photography stores or art stores that sell photography equipment in bigger cities, or in cities with art colleges. Lots of photography students means they all need to buy film, paper, cameras, and more. Electronics stores also usually have a camera department, which sells digital cameras and their accessories.

Keep in mind that it is very hard to make a lot of money as a photographer. Lots of photographers have second jobs that help them earn a living while leaving them enough time to make the art they love. Most photographers don't make very much money at all their first year or two charging money for their pictures or their photography skills. But if they keep at, some photographers end up being very successful.

Maintaining good relationships with clients who purchase your photos is key to running a successful photography business.

KEY CUSTOMERS

Who buys photography depends on what sort of business they're buying from. Each sort of photography business focuses on a different set of customers.

For example, if a photographer is uploading her images to a stock photo website, customers are likely to be other businesspeople. Businesses are looking for images to add to their own websites, or their reports, or flyers. Book and magazine publishers often use stock photos too.

Artistic photographers are usually looking to sell to individuals who want to buy art for their homes. They might start out by selling photos to friends and families, and as their business expands, they start selling to anyone who wants to buy a print. Art photographers may also target businesses that need art in their stores or offices.

Some photographers specialize in one sort of photography. An event photographer is looking for customers who are planning a wedding or other large event and who want to document it with photos. Family photographers might have their own photo studios; they work with customers who want family or child portraits.

DOROTHEA LANGE

Photographer Dorothea Lange worked at a number of different photography jobs during her artistic career. She even made money as a photographer during the Great Depression, when millions of others were without work.

Lange was born in 1895 in New Jersey. She grew to love art as a child, although schoolwork never really appealed to her. She decided to become a photographer and studied photography at Columbia University in New York. Next, she became an *apprentice* to several photographers, in order to learn the business of photography.

Research Project

Take a look at some photo businesses online. First, do a search for some stock photo websites and read up on how photographers can contribute to these sites. Then search for individual businesses run by photographers. You might find event photographers, equipment vendors, and many others. Make a list of the pros and cons of each kind of business. Which option (or options) seems like the best choice? Why?

After her apprenticeships, she opened up her own photography studio in San Francisco, California. Then, in the 1930s, the Great Depression hit. The stock market crashed, and many people lost their jobs. Lange spent a lot of time taking pictures of the effects of the Great Depression on the people around her. She took pictures of homeless people and of people waiting in bread lines. She was a skilled photographer, and pretty soon the right people noticed her. The Resettlement Authority, a part of the federal government, hired her to continue documenting what was going on in the country.

Lange took her most famous photo, "Migrant Mother," at a migrant worker camp in California. The woman in the photograph, along with her kids, had little food left to eat. Lange took her picture and her story back to a newspaper in San Francisco. The photo helped show the country what was really going on during those times. Later on, Lange took shots of people being rounded up for the Japanese internment camps that Ansel Adams also photographed.

Lange wasn't done with her photography career when the Depression ended. She became a professor of fine art photography at the California School of Fine Arts. She also started a photography magazine

Text-Dependent Questions

1. Explain how photographers make money through stock photo websites.
2. Where are two places an art photographer might choose to show his work?
3. What's an alternative job to selling photos, if someone still wants to work with photography?
4. According to the sidebar, who are three types of people artists should know if they're looking to get ahead in photography?
5. What sort of customer is likely to buy individual photos being sold by a photographer?

called *Aperture*. She kept taking photos that were shown in magazines like *Life*, and in galleries around the country.

Not every photographer's career will look like Lange's, of course. She was lucky enough to get the training she needed and a job that sponsored her photographic work. Contributing to magazines and becoming art professors are only two of the possibilities for building a career in photography. Whatever route you take, plan on it taking lots of hard work!

Words to Understand

potential: Having the ability to become something in the future.

custom design: A unique design made especially for one customer.

Chapter Four

How Can I Get Involved in Photography?

If you dream of becoming a professional photographer, you'll have to make a real-life plan before you can reach your goal. First and most important, you'll need to get really good at taking pictures. Then learn everything you can about the business of photography. Making it big in the photography world can be hard—but exciting!

LEARN THE ART

To become a photographer, you have to learn how to take pictures, of course! You should take some time to think about whether you want to start with film or digital photography. You'll learn some of the same

Getting online to research your many options for a career in photography is a good first step toward becoming a professional photographer.

tricks for taking pictures with each, but you'll learn different methods for processing and retouching photos depending on which type of photography you're practicing.

You have a few options for how to learn photography. You might be lucky enough that your school offers an art class in photography. Or maybe there's a community art school in your town or city that offers art classes. Start with a beginner class if you're new to photography, and then work your way up to intermediate and advanced classes. You can try out different types of photography to see which you like best.

You can also start teaching yourself. If all you have is a phone camera or a relatively inexpensive digital camera, start with that. You can learn how to choose objects and scenes to photograph, how to fit them into your frame, when to zoom, and more skills you'll need for creating beautiful photographs. Read up on photography online, or check out books from the library. If you get more serious about photography, you can start saving up for a better camera.

You'll need access to various equipment. Obviously, you need some sort of camera. You also need film if you're using a film camera. You can choose to send your film away to get processed, but if you want to learn all there is about film photography, you'll also need access to a dark room. Sometimes you can find a community dark room to use. You pay a small fee, and you can share the darkroom's equipment and facilities with other members.

If you're pursuing digital photography, you'll need access to image editing software. Software is often very expensive, but you don't always have to buy it yourself. Libraries occasionally have some loaded onto their computers, or you can find friends with it on their computers. Online, you should also be able to find cheaper or even free versions of image editing software that can get you started.

No matter how you learn, you'll need to practice a lot. Taking good pictures can be hard at first. You'll need to try out different lighting,

Creating an online portfolio can be a great way to show other people your work—including potential employers or customers.

different objects, and different distances to find out what works best for you. You might find that you really enjoy taking pictures of people, or nature, or buildings.

MAKE A PORTFOLIO

Portfolios are collections of an artist's work. They offer a way for other people to see a wide array of all the pieces that an artist has worked on. For photographers, portfolios usually consist of examples of photographic series they've done. Portfolios are important for job interviews, trying to land gallery shows, and to show customers.

Portfolios are usually presented on paper, but they can also be created online. Physical portfolios should include photos printed on high-quality paper so that they look as nice as possible.

A portfolio is a little more than just a bunch of pictures put together. You should also include a short statement about your work: What sort of message are you trying to get across with your work? Why do you take photos? Also include a list of all the shots and their titles and dates. A thumbnail overview of every picture in the portfolio is also a good idea. All together, a professional-looking portfolio will help convince people you're a great photographer!

CREATING A BUSINESS PLAN

If you want to start your own photography business, you'll have to plan ahead. Diving right into a business without a roadmap is almost never a good idea.

Deciding to start a photography business doesn't mean you'll be just taking and editing pictures all day. You have to spend a lot of time developing your business. To start off, you'll need a business plan, which provides a guide for your business. You can always change it later, but a business plan helps you figure out what you want your business to look like right off the bat. A business plan should include:

Learning the ins and outs of photography means taking time to study the basics, from lighting to framing. To succeed in a photography career, you need to know a lot about your art.

Make Connections

Taking good pictures again and again takes practice. Here are some tips on how to start taking your photos to the next level:

- Rule of Thirds. Resist the urge to center the main focus of your photo. Instead, imagine the picture you're taking divided into nine equal boxes. Some of the best photos have their points of interest placed along the lines that make up the boxes, or at the corners of the boxes. Properly off-centered images are more balanced and look more professional.
- Pay attention to light and exposure. Your camera might adjust to light automatically, but it doesn't always get the exposure right. Try adjusting it yourself—a longer exposure makes dark images lighter, while a shorter exposure makes too-bright images darker.
- Don't take pictures into the sun. Keep the sun at your back, and your pictures won't appear all washed out.
- Keep your distance if you're using a flash. Sometimes flashes just wash everything out in the picture, if you're too close. Back up to take your picture if you need the flash, and try zooming in on your subject instead.
- Experiment with different heights. Taking pictures at eye-level can get boring, so try taking pictures from up high or crouch down low to get more interesting shots.

- Summary. If someone doesn't have enough time to read the whole plan, she can just read the summary to get a quick overview.
- Objectives/goals. What specific, concrete things do you want to accomplish—and by when?
- General company description. Write down your mission (the reason your business exists), your form of ownership (like sole

It's never too early to start a career in photography. Get started learning about the art and business of taking photographs now to prepare yourself for a creative career in the future.

proprietorship, limited liability company, or corporation), customer audience, and business strengths.

- Industry description. What does the photography industry look like right now, and how do you fit in?
- Product/service description. Explain what sort of photographs and services you'll offer, and how much you'll charge.
- Marketing plan. You'll need to know how you're going to advertise or otherwise get people to know your business.
- Competition. Who will you be competing with in the business world? What makes you stand out?
- Distribution. Make sure you know how you'll get the final product to your customers.

Business plans make running businesses a lot easier. People with plans have clarified what they want out of a business and what it will look like. They're a step ahead of everyone else.

TAKE IT ONLINE

To have a successful business, you need a strong "online presence," as they say in business language. Having a website is really important, along with a Facebook page, and maybe a Twitter account and LinkedIn profile. People will probably find out about your business through your website or through social media. If they hear about you from a friend by word of mouth, they'll want to check out your business online first before deciding to hire you.

Your website should have lots of examples of your work. **Potential** customers will want to see what sort of pictures you take. This is where quality is important. Although a lot of business involves marketing, a good website, and good people skills, you also have to have a good product or service. All your practice and skill taking pictures will show, helping to convince people your business is worth it.

Sharing your photos is as easy as logging onto websites like Flickr.com. On these websites, you can share your photos for free, helping you to get a start in the world of photography.

Make Connections

 Small business owners need to get licenses to legally open their business and start selling to customers. Photographers mostly have to worry about local licensing at the town or city level. Check out your city's website to figure out how to get a license. Usually it involves a small fee and some paperwork, and isn't a big deal. In a few cases, the city doesn't require that some small businesses get a license.

If you know how to design a website form scratch, great! But there are plenty of options for people who don't. Wordpress, Wix, and Tumblr are all good possibilities. They let you **custom design** your own site from templates. You can include all the information you need, plus all your photos.

As a photographer, you should also think about having a Flickr site. Flickr allows people to share their photos so that anyone on Flickr can see them. And since a lot of other photographers, business people, and potential customers are on Flickr, you're showing a whole lot of people your work. If they like what they see, they can contact you directly.

ADVERTISE

Now you need to get the word out that you're in business. Tell everyone you know, invite all your friends on Facebook to like your business' page, and think about advertising. You should also think about the specific type of customer you're trying to attract and where they might go. If you're thinking about a wedding photography business, you could try and advertise in wedding dress shops, for example. Or if you want to

Make sure to stick with your passion through discouraging feedback or a lost opportunity. If you think you can make it in the world of photography, hold on to your dream even when times are hard.

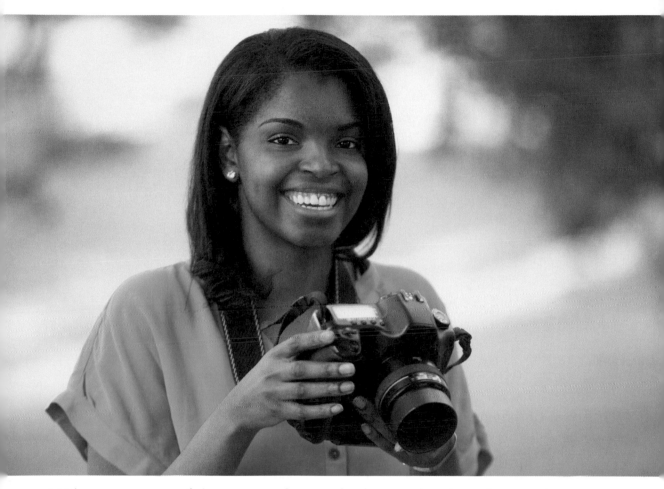

With so many ways of sharing your photos with other people online, it's easier than ever to get started in a dream career in photography. But that doesn't mean it's easy to find success. It still takes hard work to succeed in professional photography.

take pictures of people's pets, advertise with local veterinarians and dog groomers.

You have lots of advertising options. You can post flyers in local businesses' windows. You can put an add in a newspaper in print or online. You can do some research on search engine optimization (SEO) to get your website more notice online.

Text-Dependent Questions

1. What equipment do you need if you're going to pursue film photography? What equipment is necessary for digital photography?
2. How might you decide to learn photography if your school doesn't offer any photography classes?
3. What should you include in a portfolio besides examples of your art?
4. Describe at least three sections a business plan needs to be useful.
5. Why is having a website for your work important?

One trick some businesspeople use is to advertise discounts for customer referrals. If your customer refers someone to you, she gets a discount on her next purchase. Or you can offer a discount for a first-time customer, to convince him to use your photography services instead of someone else's.

KEEP AT IT

Don't expect to become the world's best photographer or an ultra-successful businessperson right away. Photography and the business of photography take time. Patience, hard work, luck, and skill all come into play.

So if you're just starting out with taking some basic pictures, give it time. As long as you practice taking pictures, take classes, and do some reading about photography, you'll see yourself improving week after week.

Research Project

Do some more research on business plans and see if you can find a useful template that makes creating one a little easier. Create a short plan for a business you might want to start. You can make up an imaginary photography business, or choose another business that interests you. Make sure you include all the important information. Make some things up if you have to, based on what you'd like your business to look like.

Millions of people have learned to be photographers since the invention of the modern camera. Whether they used a film camera, a phone camera, or a fancy digital camera, and whether they took family portraits, landscape shots, or documented social injustices, photographers have created thoughtful, memorable art. The art world—and our personal lives—would probably be very different without photography!

Find Out More

Online

BetterPhoto for Young Adults
www.betterphoto.com/photography-for-kids.asp

For Dummies: Photography and Video
www.dummies.com/how-to/photography-video.html

National Geographic Photography
photography.nationalgeographic.com/photography

The National Portrait Gallery: Photographic Techniques and Processes
www.npg.si.edu/exh/brady/intro/cont4.htm

Picture Correct: Top Ten Most Famous Photographers of All Time
www.picturecorrect.com/tips/top-10-most-famous-photographers-of-all-time

In Books

Ang, Tom. *How to Photograph Absolutely Everything: Successful Pictures From Your Digital Camera*. New York: DK Publishing, 2007.

Campbell, Marc and Dave Long. *Digital Photography for Teens*. Boston, Mass.: Thomson Course Technology, 2007.

Gilbert, George and Pamela Fehl. *Career Opportunities in Photography*. New York: Ferguson Publishing, 2006.

Sandler, Martin W. *Photography: An Illustrated History*. New York: Oxford University Press, 2002.

Styr, Charlie and Maria Wakem. *Click: the Ultimate Photography Guide for Generation Now*. New York: Amphoto Books, 2009.

Series Glossary of Key Terms

Abstract: Made up of shapes that are symbolic. You might not be able to tell what a piece of abstract art is just by looking at it.

Classical: A certain kind of art traditional to the ancient Greek and Roman civilizations. In music, it refers to music in a European tradition that includes opera and symphony and that is generally considered more serious than other kinds of music.

Culture: All the arts, social meanings, thoughts, and behaviors that are common in a certain country or group.

Gallery: A room or a building that displays art.

Genre: A category of art, all with similar characteristics or styles.

Impressionism: A style of painting that focuses more on the artist's perception of movement and lighting than what something actually looks like.

Improvisation: Created without planning or preparation.

Medium (media): The materials or techniques used to create a work of art. Oil paints are a medium. So is digital photography.

Pitch: How high or low a musical note is; where it falls on a scale.

Portfolio: A collection of some of the art an artist has created, to show off her talents.

Realism: Art that tries to show something exactly as it appears in real life.

Renaissance: A period of rapid artistic and literary development during the 1500s–1700s, or the name of the artistic style from this period.

Studio: A place where an artist can work and create his art.

Style: A certain way of creating art specific to a person or time period.

Technique: A certain way of creating a piece of art.

Tempo: How fast a piece of music goes.

Venue: The location or facility where an event takes place.

Index

About the Author

Sara James is a writer and blogger. She writes educational books for children on a variety of topics, including health, history, and current events.

Picture Credits

Dreamstime.com:
- 6: Richard Gunion
- 8: Oleksandr Lysenko
- 12: Carlos Caetano
- 14: Quentin Bargate
- 18: Adistock
- 20: Marcin Chodorowski
- 22: Jorg Hackemann
- 24: Radekdrewek
- 30: Kguzel
- 32: Heysues23
- 34: Udra11
- 35: Tomatika
- 36: Valentin Armianu
- 38: Nikolay Mamluke
- 40: Mystock88photo
- 44: Jeff Clow
- 46: Khorzhevska
- 48: Silvertiger
- 50: Oleksandr Lysenko
- 52: Robert Kneschke
- 54: Lucian Milasan
- 56: Andrei Kuzmik
- 57: Andreblais